Why Sales People Fail: It All Boils Down to One Thing

Category: Business & Economics

Author: Bob Oros

Publisher: Bob Oros Publishing

ISBN: 978-1-387-19809-2

Copyright 2017

I0475590

Description: The odds are against you, you may not make it. The light at the end of the tunnel goes out for many "would-be" sales people. They sold themselves on the idea that they were not "cut out to be in sales." They saw only the glamour of being independent with opportunity to earn "easy" money. Learn the one thing it takes to succeed in this competitive career.

Key words: motivating sales people, job in sales, sales manager training, sales course, manufacturing sales training, wholesale sales training, online sales training, distributor sales training, food sales jobs, food service sales, sales coaching, sales techniques,

ISBN 978-1-387-19809-2

90000

9 781387 198092

WHY SALES PEOPLE FAIL: IT ALL BOILS DOWN TO ONE THING

1. Why do so many sales people fail?

The odds are against you - you may not make it.

Why do so many people come into selling and after a year or two they are gone? Why do sales people fail?

Here are the reasons that sound good. These reasons justify, in the failures mind, the decision that selling is not for them. These reasons justify their failure.

"This is not worth it."

"There must be a better way to make a living."

"I'm going back to school and get a real job."

"All the good territories are already taken."

"The competition is ruthless."

"I'm going to try selling a different line."

"They expect too much."

"How can they expect me to sell anything at these prices?"

The light at the end of the tunnel went out for these "would-be" sales people. They sold themselves on the idea that they were not "cut out to be in sales."

They saw only the glamour of being independent with opportunity to earn "easy" money. Do any of these reasons sound familiar? Yes- of course they do. We have all had these thoughts at some point.

So why does one person become an outstanding success at selling while another, with the same potential, fail?

You are parked behind a restaurant sitting in your car waiting for your appointment time. The person you are going to see is probably much older and more experienced than you.   He is more than likely going to ask you something about your product line that you can't answer or don't know. As you are waiting, the anxiety grows. It is the middle of summer and the August sun is beating down on the pavement. As you get out of the car the heat and humidity are so thick you can cut it with a knife.

Let's say you are calling on a local restaurant to sell them your website service. You walk past the dumpster and the smell practically makes you sick. As you open the door the heat from the kitchen hits you like a blast furnace. The person you are going to talk to is busy working. You know he sees you but he does not make eye contact with you. He is making you stand there as if you are invisible. At this moment in time the truth will reveal itself – are you, or are you not, going to succeed in a business with such a high failure rate? At this moment you will know how well you understand the principles and psychology of the buyer/seller relationship, or simply "The Principles of Selling."

If you DO NOT understand the PRINCIPLES your reaction is predictable. You get humiliated. Upset. Embarrassed. Mad. You take the prospects rudeness as a personal insult.

Your ego gets wounded and your mind starts filling up with negative thoughts. When he finally turns to talk to you, your attitude is reflected in your face. You try to get control of your attitude – but it's too late. The prospect won in the first round!

If you DO understand the PRINCIPLES your reaction is also predictable. You understand that you are a sales person and the prospect is on the defensive. They are afraid you are going talk them into something they do not want.

They are afraid you have a certain power over them and that is why they are ignoring you. By understanding the PRINCIPLES you know that the customer is simply setting the stage and sending you a message – a message that says he is important, his time is valuable, he is in control of this meeting. By understanding the PRINCIPLES you do not let the situation turn negative.

You say to yourself "I really love what I do – I love my profession."

"I really love playing the selling game."

"He's made his first move and he is doing it quite well."

"When he does acknowledge me I will greet him with a smile and an attitude of appreciation for letting me talk to him."

Do you see the difference? So, what is the reason so many sales people fail? Here is the reason – read it carefully.

The person who fails usually has been thoroughly trained in the products and services they are going to sell - they have NOT been trained in the psychology and principles of selling.

Sounds simple, I know.

Most non-selling managers and business owners believe that successful sales people are born that way. This is simply not true. A sales person needs professional training just as much as a doctor, lawyer, airline pilot, accountant, carpenter or chef. Why should selling be any different?

Successful sales people learn the principles of selling and apply them. Sales people who fail do not learn the principles of selling and rely on their ability to "wing it", which ultimately lets them down. We have already touched on an important principle.

ATTITUDE MANAGEMENT.

Not just having a positive attitude – but managing your attitude under all the various selling situations. Programming your mind to react in a certain way in a specific situation. It does no good to read about something as important as attitude management and then do nothing about it.

To manage your attitude you must monitor your thoughts and feelings under every selling situation. Approach it as if you were doing a scientific study. When you find that you are reacting negatively to a specific situation, you have found an opportunity to sharpen your skill.

For a mental picture of this concept think back to some of the old Star Trek shows. Captain Kirk represented the conscious mind, McCoy represented the emotional side and Spok represented the logical side. The key was in the balance.

Comments and suggestions from sales professionals.

I have to keep reminding myself throughout my day that my attitude is what shapes my next move. If I were to get myself down by every negative situation that happens in my life, It would certainly start to lose meaning. In selling to someone, dealing with No's is an everyday occurrence. I find it difficult sometimes because I am only trying to help and if given the opportunity, the customer would see that.

Yes, I am also selling my products, but I am only helping the customer get the best products at the best deals and most of the time when they don't give you the time of day, it puts a damper in the mood because they don't know me and what I stand for, and if they did, the outcome would be a lot different.

But again, I have a choice to whom I want to sell to and I to keep reminding myself that not every customer I want to have a relationship with. So for me, the ones that do give me the time of day, that's who gets the benefit of a relationship and the attitude that I choose to have day in and day out.

Joshua Borges

Moving from 25 years as a restaurant operator with 10 of that as an owner into a "sales" position the attitude is what I recognize as my challenge. I know what that purchaser is thinking when I walk in and I don't want to be "that guy." My objective is to make myself an asset for them and not an "issue".

Phil de Gruy

I believe a first impression and positive attitude that will set the stage for the sales call. You only have a small window to win the customer over in the first few minutes of the meeting. You have to know why you are going in to visit the customer. Think of the customer as part of your family.
Jim Harris

If you give up after being told no you won't be in this business very long.   You have to learn the art of listening. Not just hear what a buyer is saying but listen and fill in the parts that he doesn't tell you. Once you master this art you will successfully cross from being a sales person to a consultant. It doesn't happen overnight and you need to develop a thick skin along the way. Once a buyer sees this trait in you he will have the confidence to trust and enter into a business relationship with you.
Randy Knotts

Attitude and energy are what it takes. You have make it part of the muscle memory in the brain to turn the other cheek with a smile. I tell myself my biggest competitor is me. If I am not selling someone it is because I don't want to or I have not put forth the effort too. It is not the big that eat the small it is the fast and more prepared that eat the slow and unprepared.

Jim Clark

I must admit that in the past I have been a little negative on a sales career. This goes back to my past when I took one of those summer jobs when I was back in college in the early 1970's selling encyclopedias for a company that used deceptive trade practices. Basically you went door to door and lied to people for the company telling you were taking a marketing survey.   After 2 weeks of that and making no money and encounters with the police for door to door soliciting [which was illegal in Baton Rouge,La and the company didn't inform me on that till the police came] my high moral values took over and I quit. The company was later charged by the Federal Government for deceptive trade practices and paid rather a hefty fine.

Cary McAfee

I find that a lot of sales people get weighed down with the "No" even before they go into the account. When I first started in this business, after a day of no's, I was telling my wife about my day and how I know I could help these customers, but they keep 'looking at me as if I'm a lair'!

Her response was, "What do you expect you are a salesman". From that moment on I became a 'consultant', one with an answer to a customer's needs.

Another thing that add to the failure rate, is not understanding that a 'no' on Monday a 9:00 AM, may not be a 'no' on Thursday at 2:00 PM …. You got to keep listening for an need and address (sale) around those needs.

David Vize

I had not a clue those marketing classes I chose as electives in college would help me today. Through those lectures we were taught always to investigate the business you are pursuing. Knowing what the business is about and what their initiative is, getting to understand the person behind the business, and networking with people who are already involved with the business. Also, never let your guard down and always be a positive thinker and speaker. Any form of negativity could affect the bond or connection you are trying to build with a prospective client. Something I know that has helped me over the years especially in customer service is that old phrase "Kill them with kindness."

Shawn Hollis

Some of the most satisfying experiences in sales for me have been succeeding with the "tough" customer, the one who initially seems to not like you and considers you to be a waste of his time. When you eventually win him over, he many times becomes a strong, long term ally.

Crocker Smith

I believe that if you show a positive persona, believe in that positive persona, then everyone (including customers) will begin to feed off your positive attitude. Try this: the next time you meet a person for the first time or see someone that you haven't seen in a few days, and they ask "how are you?" Use the response "GREAT!!!" with an explosive, over joyous and big smile and see if you don't get a smile back. It may not be genuine but at least you're not giving off a negative or downtrodden attitude. Of Course, the person is going to ask you what makes your day so great....my response? "I woke up breathing, everything else is

irrelevant." I guess It comes down to "Carpe Diem." Make the very best of every day. A positive attitude is contagious as well as a negative one. Which is the better?

Tim Hopkins

"The longer I live, the more I realize the impact of attitude on life. Attitude, to me, is more important than facts.

It is more important than the past, than education, than money, than circumstances, than failures, than successes, than what other people think or say or do. It is more important than appearance, giftedness, or skill. It will make or break a company.....a church....a home.

The remarkable thing is we have a choice every day regarding the attitude we will embrace for that day. We cannot change our past.......we cannot change the fact that people will act in a certain way. We cannot change the inevitable. The only thing we can do is play on the one string we have, and that is our attitude.....

I am convinced that life is 10% what happens to me and 90% how I react to it. And so it is with you …. We are in charge of our Attitudes."

Charles Swindole

I totally understand the intimidating factor in selling. I have felt that in environments I was not familiar with. Fortunately, with my experience as a restaurant general manager, I totally feel comfortable standing in a kitchen or in the front because it gives me the opportunity to see all the different ways I can help them and just gives me more ammunition to at them with. If an owner / manager gives me this opportunity I will always find something I can speak with them about. I have also learned you will never get good at this unless you step out of your comfort zone and challenge yourself. A positive attitude goes a long way in winning over a prospective customer, and a willingness to listen to their challenges and being willing to step in the middle and offer solutions.

Donnie Little

Hmmmmmm...................attitude management. Seems like a no brainer. It really comes down to control. And of course with our under developed cerebral cortex our emotions are often the most difficult aspects of our personalities to be in control of. Emotional control is the key to being in control of almost any situation. If you can train yourself to control your thoughts and feelings, or at least your reaction to those thoughts and feelings you will always have the upper hand and your "adversary" (who will hopefully over time become your partner in this sales relationship) will never even realize they are slowly being recruited to your "side". "Never let em see you sweat".

Kirk Jones

"You only get the opportunity to a first impression once. There are no "do overs" on how you CHOOSE to initially present yourself. People need to see something in you that they want to have before you ever try to "sell" anything."

Lynn Mosely

"There is no one more valuable than a sales person with confidence. The ability to show a confident persona is the best way to make the customer believe you have the solution to their problem."

Drew Culbreth

2. What is the most important sale you have to make?

What is the one thing that keeps you from making sales, keeps you worrying about business, and keeps you feeling insecure?

I am going to identify it but first, let me assure you, everyone is affected by it. Regardless of how long you have been in sales or how many setbacks you have to face.

Here is the hardest thing you have to do. You have to see in your mind not the way things are, but the way things can become.

This is easy to do when things are going along smooth. When customers are buying, progress is being made and things are looking pretty good. When you are in the "success frame of mind" it is easy to see all the possibilities. However, when you are up against tough times is when you are tested. That is when you really find out how difficult it is to see things the way you want them to become. Especially when you look around and you are in a seemingly impossible situation.

The law of nature insists that you grow. When you are growing and improving you are naturally positive and excited about what you are doing.

However, when you run into an obstacle and you go backwards, just the opposite takes place. All of a sudden you see yourself filled with apprehension and failure.

Lets see how good of a sales person you really are. Lets see if you can make a sale to yourself. Let's see if you can design and present a program to yourself that will get you excited about sales in spite of what everyone is saying about the economy.

Here is a common mistake most people make when they lay out a program for themselves, which you may be guilty of as well. You have been focusing on the FEATURES when you set your goals. The FEATURES are boring. The FEATURES will never get you excited. You have to give yourself a BENEFIT presentation!

In case you are not clear on the difference between a FEATURE and a BENEFIT, a feature is a fact about the product or service, a benefit is what it does.

For example the feature of a Ford Truck is that it has a V10 450 horse power engine. The benefit is that it will pull a 10,000 pound trailer up a steep hill with ease. The

BENEFIT is SEEING yourself driving the truck and pulling your RV or boat up the hill without any trouble.

Personal goal setting is important. What is even more important are the BENEFITS you will personally receive once your objectives are reached.

Here's what I mean. Owning your home free and clear is not a goal, but a benefit of reaching your sales and commission objective.

The extra money you want to put in your retirement account is not a goal, it is the benefit of reaching your sales objective.

Paying off your credit cards is not a goal, but a benefit of reaching your sales objective.

You talk to your customers about the benefits of your products and services - why not make the same case for selling yourself on your own personal success? Why do you want to be successful?

Lack of goal setting is rarely a problem. You either set them yourself, or your company sets them for you. Goals in themselves rarely have enough power to motivate you.

What will motivate you are the personal BENEFITS you get from accomplishing your goal. Your goal as a sales person is simple: Exceed your sales plan. If you have identified the BENEFITS you really want badly enough to take action you will be motivated. If you have not clearly identified your benefits you will not be motivated.

Exceeding your sales plan is a FEATURE not a BENEFIT. What are benefits you receive when you exceed your sales objective?

Once the benefits are listed, you will have your "reason why." You will find the personal motivation that gets you out the door early. The motivation to overcome call reluctance. The motivation to make the extra call. The motivation to ask for the additional business.

Your single goal is to exceed your sales plan. Stop now. Take out a piece of paper. Make a list of the BENEFITS you will enjoy by exceeding your sales plan. List all the BENEFITS you will receive once you exceed this goal. Better yet, get some pictures that represent the benefits and picture yourself as already having achieved them.

Growth is the purpose of life. If you are not growing you are simply taking up space. To make progress you have to grow until you become larger than your current situation.

This attitude of GROWTH in a sales person is imperative. You MUST have it. You MUST want more. You MUST be aggressive with your actions and demand a lot from yourself. You must be able to "see" things the way they can become, not the way they are.

This is the key of a motivated sales person. A believer. A person who knows what they want. A person who is willing to pay the price. A person who has a "reason why."

You must have plan going forward in life. No different than having a plan for your customers. They also want to know what their BENEFIT is to deal YOU. Knowing your BENEFITS every morning when you are walking out the door for work, will motivate you to close that sale. Yes with positive attitude and knowing your BENEFITS will get me that BIG Boat that I have always wanted.

Jim Harris

What an awesome way to focus the plan on achievement! To keep our eyes on the benefits we will receive! If we get that mental image it will be very motivating. I see myself lying on the beach in the Virgin Islands as a size 6.

Tanzie Zizza

I'm amazed how easy it is to get hung up on the Features, when all of us really aim for the Benefits. Once I defined Benefits to myself as Time / Money, then I was able to grab onto a quirky thought, which is achieve the Benefit of my set goal and then the goal is FREE with a little hard work. Our family of 4 had the best cruise on the Mexican Riviera for our 20th Wedding Anniversary, and it only cost $20,000.00! That's right, 3 years hard work, and not a dime out of our daily expenses.

Mark Brackett

A very common figure of speech about goal setting is take it "one day at a time". In sales this really does not work unless you have a plan done in advance. The work of today does not normally see the benefits for months, sometimes even years. I like your idea of the 90 day plan. Which I am going to try, I currently follow a monthly, weekly and daily plan. Nothing makes me feel more confident than leaving my house each morning knowing exactly where I am going and what my plan is for each stop.

Candy Swift

The only motivation I need to get me going in the morning is my responsibility to my family and wanting to be the best for them and myself. It is my desire to not let them down that pushes me to do everything I can to improve our lives together. That means doing my planning, focusing on exceeding my sales objectives and staying out there and exceeding our customers expectations when it is easy just to pack it in. Some of my best success stories have come after the end of a business day. I understand motivation is the single most challenging aspect of being in sales. Each of us needs to find that sense of purpose to be successful. If it is our family or some other motivating factor, we must have something that will give us a sense of purpose to succeed.

Donnie Little

I agree it does take time to become a successful sales person. Anyone can be a salesperson; it just depends on what your idea of successful is. Some think its getting a couple new sales every couple months. To me being a successful salesperson means making new contacts every day while maintaining the current relationships. When you do that you will have much more than a couple of sales. Three years seems to be accurate as it takes time to learn what works and what doesn't, you cant always follow the lead of others. What works for them may not work for you.

Brandon Sanchez

When one is MATURE, they will have achieved the status of SALES PROFESSIONAL. This status is not achieved on a watch or a calendar. However, it does take time to gain maturity. In order to achieve maturity (and professionalism) certain actions MUST be taken. First, effective planning, i.e., Plan your work and work your plan. Second, Profit from experience, both good and bad. One's own experiences will serve as their best teacher. Third, set and achieve personal goals. Don't set your goals so low that you are not challenged but don't set them so high that they are impossible to reach. Reasonable goals are usually agreed upon by sales professionals and sales managers. For the free agent, their spouse can usually assist by presenting a WANT LIST at the beginning of each year.

Mike Dame

I feel like in order to be successful in anything you must take things one day and one step at the time. You must have patience, and determination to accomplish your goals.

Working on the overall goal on a daily basis. Don't rush, take on one task at the time, and stay focused. By doing this daily you can accomplish anything you set you mind to do.

Laura Rice

This definitely relates to the old adage "PLAN YOUR WORK, AND WORK YOUR PLAN!" Within the selling industry, you must allow for flexibility and schedules to change (i.e. broken appointments, no shows, things of that nature), but you also must include a certain amount of rigidity within your schedule. If you don't have a plan, and don't have written goals set, how will you know if you ever reach them. How will you know if you ever succeed?

Scott Green

In repeat selling it generally takes 2-3 years for the salesperson to gain the customer's trust and confidence. People are slow to let down their defenses, and rightfully so. But once you have gained this trust your life is a lot easier.

Also, having a mentor to guide a new salesperson dramatically speeds up the learning process – an experienced and successful salesperson to help navigate you through the learning minefield.

Crocker Smith

3. Why do most motivation programs fail?

Do you have a good education? Do you know more about your products than anybody? Have you read every book you can find on selling? Do you listen to motivational CDs while driving? Do you read all the trade journals? Do you attend seminars and take pages of notes? Do you ask successful sales people for advice?

If you do - IT DOESN'T MATTER! That's right!

You may be fooling yourself and maybe some of your colleagues into thinking you are really going places. But it doesn't really matter. I am going to tell you to do something that is going to shock your system.

Take all your motivational CDs and burn them!

 Take your library of selling books to the dump!

 Take your list of big impressive goals and tear it up!

 Why would I make a statement like that?

Why would I give you that kind of advice? Because I am trying to help you. I want you to be more successful. You see, in sales, none of those things really make much difference. Here is what I mean.

Read this next paragraph carefully.

...You can have a great amount of knowledge

...read all types of positive thinking books

...listen to motivation and self help CDs

...write down big impressive goals and plans

...and be no farther ahead than a year ago

...unless you apply what you know!

UNLESS YOU APPLY WHAT YOU KNOW!

I am not saying that it is not a great accomplishment to have a degree or it is not important to listen to motivation CDs. I mean that many folks fail in sales because they don't apply what they learn. They never use the information to for their personal motivation.

Once you start to DO the things necessary for success you will find that you have what it takes. You will never know where you need to improve until you put yourself in front of the buyer and let him or her tell you the reasons they are not going to buy. You will then have experience. You will then have specific information to work on. You will then be able to put together a plan of attack based on actual feedback.

Take it from someone who does all those things. And it doesn't make me an additional dime. Unless I take one specific skill or strategy at a time and APPLY IT!

Knowledge is not the answer. The answer to personal motivation is...

APPLICATION of specific knowledge.

APPLICATION OF THE PRINCIPLES OF SELLING.

If you read something that you remember reading in the past, ask yourself this:

Did I apply it - or did I just read it?

I couldn't agree more. I have read books and attended seminars. I have been "pumped up" by motivators and been paid hard cash money for "correct answers." At the end of the day I was mostly confused and worn out. More importantly I doubted how I had approached customers and applied the techniques of selling in my own style. This only led to several days of frustration trying out these new magic selling strategies. Today I ask myself before and after every call if what I did or could do worked the best and if I was prepared for the sales call. Most importantly I don't follow someone else's script.

Dave Ferren

Smothering yourself with books, motivational tapes, and tons of training material is only putting off the inevitable....Facing the Customer. It is an excuse to not have to go out into the real world. It's like being in college in this controlled atmosphere...it makes it look easy, but until you are right in the middle of it you will not learn half as much or grow near as fast.

Liz Vaughan

It is critical to convert sales knowledge into your own style where you will be comfortable and natural in front of a customer. Customers are quick to pick up on and are turned off by a "canned" delivery or a delivery that does not match your personality. Some sales people are very effective with a hard, fast approach while others do very well with a more laid back tone. Trying to be something you are not usually does not work.

Crocker Smith

I agree you need to apply what you know. I compare it to: If you are serious about dieting or exercising to lose weight, it doesn't do any good to read all about while sitting on the couch in front of the TV eating chocolate.

It's easy to say what you are going to do but it can be difficult when it's time to apply it to what ever the situation is.

Vickie Reihl

If you do not apply what you read and learn, then you might as well find a job where you clock in and clock out. In college, they called it "Toilet Brains" which is: don't study hard for a test and then just "flush" it all when you finish the test. Carry the knowledge with you.

Trip English

I think that motivational programs are great in the aspect that they do plant the seed for you to do better - to achieve that next sale and to make you feel like you just won the lottery. But without applying what you have learned would be the same as taking driving lessons, and listening to your instructor teach you how to drive, but not applying what they have taught you ... you'd end up another statistic that crashes the car. It's really common sense to apply what you learn, but sometimes you lose sight of that with every day life.

Jo Welch

Applying what you know, in this segment, is methodology. Understand the selling principles, and apply them. Doing this regularly will allow it to become natural, and a non-task. Without applying the knowledge/principles of selling, there is no point of knowing them. We all know that we CAN lose weight. Many of us CAN resist that bag of chips, or the second helping - but DO we? Application is a method of ensuring we follow through. We know to keep opening account margin's up, but we are sometimes quick to drop the margin right away. In 'gross profit poker', this is tantamount to a fold.

Craig Young

If you have a sales degree, and think you are the greatest sales-person to ever walk the face of the earth, but you don't apply anything you have learned, you will soon realize that maybe you aren't all that great after-all.

Laura J. Czajka

Motivational programs are like diets.   You see people who look great and you want to look great too.

However, they had to take action… eat right and exercise to achieve their goal. Sales books and Motivational programs only provide outlines or ideas for the person listening to or reading them to follow. A book has never made a sale.

Kathie Luttrell

4. How long does it take to become a sales professional?

Why do I feel like telling them to take this job and shove it? Why am I all stressed out at the end of each selling day? More than likely it is because you haven't done your time. You haven't done your three years.

After three years in sales you will begin to feel confident. After five years it is very unlikely that you will ever want to do anything else for a living.

Take a walk through any bookstore - look at the success section. Most of the titles hint on the idea that your success is guaranteed instantly if you follow their formula.

Turn on the TV. During a commercial break notice how fast you can lose your headache - 15 seconds! These fast results create an unrealistic time frame for success in sales. When it doesn't happen instantly you get stressed out. You begin to think you are not cut out for selling. You get a bad attitude. You think about quitting.

Ask yourself this question. "How long do I think it will take to become a true professional in sales?" See how close you come to three years.

How do you make it through those long three years? It takes short term and long term planning to be successful at anything. Careful planning will develop persistence.

Start now. Commit yourself to a daily schedule. Do it one day at a time. Plan tomorrow the evening before. Prioritize your daily objectives. Make a list of all the things you want to accomplish. Rank them in the order of their importance. Be persistent with this exercise.

Set a 90 day sales goal. Work towards it every day. Don't look beyond 90 days - just focus on your first step. After you reach it - set another 90 day sales goal. Once you repeat the process 12 times you will be there.

Focus on today. On Friday evening or Saturday morning, prepare your schedule for the week to come. Don't feel you have to account for every minute of every one of the next five days. Block out your scheduled appointments and meetings so you have a good solid overview of what you are doing.

Prepare for each call you are going to make. By attending to daily scheduling matters you will have more confidence. Your self-esteem will go up. By comparing your actual results with your plan, you'll increase your time-effectiveness. At the end of the day you will feel great.

You won't feel like telling them to take this job and shove it! You will actually start having a good time.

I can agree that at least 3 years could be used as a benchmark but I personally feel that if you think that you are a sales "professional" that is when you are somewhat vulnerable. A salesperson can and should always be like a sponge in the marketplace,sales meetings or other trade related aspects to acquire as much knowledge as humanly possible. I have been a sales rep for 22 years and it still is amazing how much more that I can learn.

David Anderson

Persistence has played a big part for me in the market I am in so far and will continue the further along I get. But like some of the other posts discussed, it all depends on the individual and the time and effort they put in to it. I have also learned that organization and planning are also a big key to success, and if someone does not take the time now to do those things that three years will then be five years. So I believe persistence, organization, and planning are some of the best tools for me at this stage in my career. Then we can also add this course to my tool bag.

Jason Kirouac

Well everyone is different. And as long as you are doing your job and persistent in making the calls everyday this should help you to build up your confidence. It could take 3 years or it could take less, it all depends on how committed you are to being a salesperson and how well you want to succeed.

Jenn Snider

Well, I don't totally agree with the time frame to become a true sales professional.

What I mean is, yes, through trial and error it would take every bit of 3 years if not longer to figure out what works to be successful. However, I am a true believer in "Modeling," meaning find someone you look up to in the industry that you are involved with and follow in their foot steps. This let's you achieve ranks much faster with less errors. That's why I was so excited when I found out you were coming to do a seminar for us!

Since then I intend on having your course coach me to great success in a portion of the time that some of the veterans in the industry have taken to achieve similar results. I believe in learning from ones mistakes. But I also believe in standing on the shoulders of giants to meet the results I require of myself.

I sincerely believe that your coaching will be a true benefit in every aspect of my goals personally and financially.

Dwayne Mitchell

I would have to agree that it does take persistence to become a sales professional. As for what the actual benchmark is, I think it would vary depending on the individual. If you are committed to being a success, and you plan ahead (whether it's a day, or a week, or a month) I think that this would help to lay the ground work for becoming successful, but you also need to follow thru with your plan.

Selling definitely doesn't come from overnight studying and cramming to make it work, it comes from effectively listening to your customer and applying what they are telling you with a way that you can make it happen for them.

JoAnne Welch

5. What is the best approach to problems?

"You don't understand - my company has some big problems and it makes my job really tough!" Pick up the Sunday paper, go to the classified section and find a job that has no problems. If it is there - they don't need you. A company with problems is a company with opportunities!

A problem is a chance for you to show your best. There are people who spend all their time reinforcing obstacles. Office politics. Perceived defects in the product or service. Impossibly tough competition. Endless personal problems. Unfair commission schedules. We all have problems.

A persistent negative outlook will not only make it difficult for coworkers and supervisors to work with you--it will make it difficult for customers to work with you.

It's common to hear a salesperson complain, "you don't understand how much is expected of us here."

The goals of most sales managers are usually pretty clear-cut: get good results from the staff. If you're not making sales, complaining about everything is only going to compound the problem. Not only will you be wasting valuable time you could be using to talk to new customers, but you'll also lose the perspective you need to identify and resolve the problems you're having.

Many companies have had the experience of having a salesperson perform poorly in a certain territory, complaining that "the market is saturated". Take that person off the territory, put someone else on it, and sales take off.

Usually, the first salesperson focuses on limitations, while the new sales person brings no preconceptions to the territory, and sees fresh opportunities as a result.

The best approach to problems is to become part of the solution. Leaving one company because of problems and going to another is a trade off for new problems. No one likes to be around someone with a negative attitude. Carrying around negativity drags you down and keeps you from moving full speed ahead. A persistent positive attitude can cancel the negative one's.

It takes 4 positive actions or comments to make up for one negative action or comment. Honestly, it takes much more work to remain positive than negative. Negativity in the work environment can spread like a cancer. It starts with one member and quickly moves to other members until the whole office or company is infected. Obstacles will always be a permanent fixture of everyday life, but the bright side is there are ways around them. Satisfaction comes from being victorious over those obstacles.

Years ago I had a customer tell me that he was going to leave and go to a competitor. When I asked why he told me all the things that were wrong with my company. After he told me I realized that I was the one who told him all those things. A good lesson about saying something negative about your own company - it will always come back to bite you.

Having sales positions at two companies doing the same thing, one with a positive environment, and one that was not, I quickly noticed how much better my personal health was once I was involved with a "yes we can" environment.

Mark Brackett

Do you know the difference between an issue and a problem? Issues are discussed and problems are dealt with. I think a lot of times it is easy for a person to turn an issue into something bigger than it really is, like a problem. This is where a lot of the negativity comes from. And like you talked about in this lesson it takes 4 positive actions or comments to make up for one negative. I try to remain positive in all situations regardless if the call did not go so well. Tomorrow is a new day!

Jason Kirouac

I agree when there is negativity it takes more to get positive. When I know the problem may lay within my company my response to my customers is passion and understanding about the way they feel. Letting them know I am there for them and we will resolve it together.

 My goal is to let my customers know they are my partner and we are working towards a long and happy future together. Sometimes it's really hard to get over that negative side. I find that it helps to take a 10 minute break to clear my head and remind myself that we can't sweat the small stuff.

Sarah Jones

I learned a long time ago how badly negativity can drain you if you allow it. I was in the wrong seat working at a great company but my negativity about having to stay in a chair and work behind a computer with a headset was about to drive me stir crazy. The upper management had a negative attitude toward the company and it filtered all the way down to us worker bees.

I remember going into work and as I walked thru the office I smiled and asked everyone how they were. The majority of replies I got were negative. Once I made it to my department I asked my co-workers and got smiles and heard great things. I asked one co-worker "so are you going to ask how I'm doing today?" She said I always ask and I get the same answer. Wow, she shocked me. That's when she said to me "I love my job and this company and if you are so unhappy in your role change seats or leave the company!"

As I thought about what she said I came to the realization that my negativity was infecting her and her perception of the entire company.

Wow, I didn't want to be known as the person that infected people with negativity. I wanted to be known as the person that was happy and someone that did a great job. That's something that has stuck with me over the years.   I'm not a negative person and choose to not associate with people that aren't optimistic. I share that story when I

detect negativity towards a position, management or a company. Choose to be happy everyday; people will notice.

Becky Akins

Everyone needs to get a sign and post it on the mirror in the bathroom. It should read " Your looking at the problem!" More times than not, that would be correct! Even if you are not a negative person, when you listen to a coworker run the company down and don't say anything, you become an enabler. The best response I have found is to ask the person " What do you think we would have to do to fix this?" or " If you owned this company, how would you have handled that issue?" Sometimes it's best to suggest that they do look for other employment....even help them look!

Cee Coats

"The best approach to problems is to become part of the solution. Everyone needs to find out if the problem is a problem for them as an individual or is it a problem for the company?. I believe most individuals perceive problems as a personal problem; if they can overcome that, and discuss the situation with others (supervisor, coworkers,) sometimes a team effort may come up with a better solution. I believe that most companies attempt to work as a team-rely on that team.

The information provided indicates that a problem is a chance for a person to show their best. That is valuable!!!! I am not sure of all the answers to this question, but I do know that losing the negativity is the first step."

Jennifer Anderson

"You're absolutely right Bob, every company has problems. Leaving one company because of problems and going to another is a trade off for new problems. My motto on that is, "don't sweat the small stuff", and "it's all small stuff". No one likes to be around someone with a negative attitude. It's like swimming in muck. Carrying around negativity drags you down and keeps you from moving full speed ahead. A persistent positive attitude can cancel the negative one."

Kate Farrell

"I once heard a statement that had a profound effect on me..."It takes 4 positive actions or comments to make up for one negative action or comment". Honestly, it takes much more work to remain positive than negative. Why is that? I do not have the answer. But from lesson 5, I can tell you that negativity in the work environment can spread like a cancer. It starts with one member and quickly moves to other members until the whole office or company body is infected. Obstacles will always be a permanent fixture of everyday life, but the bright side is there are ways around them. Satisfaction comes from being victorious over those obstacles. Perseverance and optimism comes from deep within everyone's individual personal well. We just have to learn to tap into it."

Sharalene

This may be a different analogy but getting caught up in the misery of your problems is like an addict wallowing in his drug addiction. An addict will associate themselves with other addicts to make oneself feel better until he has had enough of the misery and finds a solution to live a clean life.

By identifying problems and finding solutions, salespeople can keep a positive attitude and keep an open mind that will benefit their company and their clients.

Gregg Nixon

6. How can you guarantee your success in sales?

Do you know that it is IMPOSSIBLE to fail in sales? It is impossible to persistently apply and reapply the principles of selling and fail. It can't be done!

Once again, the key is to persistently apply and reapply the principles of selling.

People don't fail because they are "not cut out" for sales. They fail because they are not willing to do the things successful people are willing to do.

Application of selling principles is the key. Many sales people talk a good game. They can tell you about the big sale they almost made, the hot new account they are working on, or the big sales goal they have. They can talk a good game with their customers as well.

"Sure, I will get back to you on that."

"Trust me, this is the product and program for you."

You know the type.

The person who continuously looks for new ideas and better methods of selling is the one who moves forward. The person who learns something new, applies it and reapplies it over and over until it becomes a skill. This doesn't have to be some "new" selling secret, it only has to be "new" to you. The basic principles of selling never change!

The person who DOES what he or she says they are going to do is the one who makes it in the long run.

Customers are not sold by empty promises made by sales people who are insincere. They are sold by a sales person who WEARS WELL. The person who looks for ways to show their customers how to make more money, how to sell more, how better manage their business, is the person who is not full of hot air and promises. They really don't SELL as much as they HELP CUSTOMERS BUY.

To be the type of person who wears well all you have to do is simply...

1. DO WHAT YOU SAY YOU WILL DO. Don't be "All Sizzle and No Steak"

2. Apply what you learn and then reapply it again and again until it is automatic.

The toughest door to open is the one that gets you out of the house early and the toughest sale is the one we have to make to yourself. You have to convince yourself to do what you learn until you own the skill, to apply what may seem difficult at first.

There is no magic rabbit that you pull out of the hat and say "here is the secret of selling." There is no silver bullet that will win the sale every time.

There are 7 basic areas of the sales process. If you focus on become an expert in each area, you will do fine.

1 Planning To get big results set big goals

2 Questions Ask questions that make the sale

3 Value Make every call an irresistible offer

4 Presentation Give reasons why they should buy

5 Objections Remove every roadblock to the sale

6 Closing Ask for the order and get paid

7 Follow up Remove all hope for competitors

It is impossible to persistently apply and reapply these 7 principles of selling and fail.

I was once told by a great football coach that practice does not make perfect. I was a little thrown by his comment because that expression is commonly used by most. He told me that perfect practice makes perfect. You can practice the wrong way and never get any better."

I appreciated the primary sales rep I used when operating my restaurant. He never brought me items he knew didn't fit my concept. Yet he was always researching things that would benefit me. His integrity is what made me stick like glue to him and his company. I NEVER SHOPPED PRICES in 10 years.

Phil de Gruy

I am a new salesman in an industry full of competition. However, if I am tough, and competent, then I will succeed. Gene Kranz, a very tough and competent mission control director for the Apollo moon program created a list of Foundations for his teams that he displayed on the mission control room walls. One of the qualities he emphasized is Confidence, which he defined as "Believing in ourselves as well as others, knowing that we must master fear and hesitation before we can succeed". This will be just one of the many methods that I will practice on my road to success.

Stephen Carney

From day one I have been told this, "do what you say you are going to do". I have stuck to it and I still could not believe some of the reactions I have received when I came back the day and time I said I would. I may not know as much as the other guys on the streets but if I show an honest interest in that customers business, follow up, and do what I said I would then there is no way I will fail.

Jason Kirouac

Most business owners are under tremendous stress everyday, worrying about a multitude of different aspects of their company. Anyone who can remove some of this stress is highly valuable to them. If you gain their trust they can stop worrying so much about that one area. You become an ally and another positive step toward their success. They will reward you.

Crocker Smith

That says it all. People believe that if you are a salesperson then you have to be full of hot air or a good liar. That is simply not true. If you follow through on what you promise your customer you will get their business now and for a long time to come.

Brandon Sanchez

You are right..... There is NOT a silver bullet. (If there was; I would be skiing in Europe right now). Persistence comes pretty close. Calculate how many no's it takes before you get a yes. Then with each No you are that much closer to your next sale.

A pleasing personality may get in the front door- your integrity will keep you there.

Teresa Cloninger

Just like a car salesman who tells you, you can have this car at this payment and when you get to the table the payment is not what he promised. This is the first indication that he does not have your best interest at heart. Which leads directly to mistrust! If you tell a customer that you can do some thing for them then do all in your power to get that do if you cant don't say you can. It will make you and your Company look bad in that clients view and the word will spread. Saying things that aren't true to your client just makes you look like your full of hot air. And an untrustworthy business associate. Apply what you learn to your business and do it on a daily bases and at some point it will began to work

Brian Spraggins

I have two rules that I live by when I am on the job, and they are also my pet peeves. The first one is I always return phone calls in a timely manner and I am real impatient with people who don't. The second is focusing on the person or client I am with. There is nothing that upsets me more than trying to do business with someone and they are constantly answering their cell phone or distracted by other things when they should be taking care of the person sitting in front of them.

Vickie Reihl

I ALWAYS stand behind my word. If I promise you something I will come through with it. Whatever advice I get I practice it on a daily bases. As my father always told me "Practice what you preach." I have found that to be so true. If you don't practice and live by it where will you be in life? Would you be a successful business person? I believe we should be consistent on what we say and promise. If we practice what we preach to our customers we will have their business for a lifetime and they will be just as loyal to us as we are to them. I found if you are loyal and persistent it pays off! Then you will exceed your expectations.

Nina Hall

Follow up and follow through. I don't believe there are any other aspects of much importance as these two in the selling business. They show the costumer you are concerned with more than just the short 15 minute sales meeting you may have had with them. It shows them that you care about what they want and it shows them that you take time out of your day to check in with them. Don't make any promises that you aren't 100% sure you can keep.

Matthew Thacker

My word is my bond – I will never promise something I'm not 100% sure I can deliver. Talking the talk and not walking is a personal pet peeve of mine and I think allot of people, specifically customers. Words are not impressive, action and follow-up makes the sell.

Danielle Antonacci

You are right. You can not fail if you are doing the right things. Here are two (2) big ones:

1. Follow up on an issue or idea the customer had. Good or bad, follow up on it. They are counting on YOU.

2. Return the phone call ! I hear this one a lot. "The last salesman or your competition does not return phone calls promptly:

I do not take my phone into accounts. If I have a sick kid or wife at home I will place my phone on vibrate.

Do not answer your phone when you are with your customer. That is your time with them, you are just interrupting your selling time.

Be careful of what you say, because you are going to back up what you said.

Follow through with what you say. If you can't get it done right away, make sure you tell the customer: "I will get right on this, but give me a few days to pull up and review the data" Don't promise it the next day if you can't deliver.

In this lesson we learned the hardest door to open is the front door to get in the car. The hardest account to call on, is the one you drove by for the past few years and have never stopped in. Use your blinker and use your brakes more often, get out of the safety zone.

I have a 1981 Jeep CJ7 and we go four-wheeling now and then. When you're out in the woods you will discover "Ruts" in the road. They can be either dry or filled with water, but when you look at them, you can tell the people before you had safe passage through these "ruts". You feel safe and confident going through the "ruts" because you know you have a better chance of making it through tough times. Sometimes you break out of the safety zone and turn your wheels and tires a different direction to get out of these ruts.

Take a different way to work, stop at that account you saw your competitor at. Use the brakes, turn the wheel !!!

Trip English

7. How do you build credibility with your customers?

Many years ago the 3M Company sent researchers to study the top sales people in the company. Their assignment was to find the EXACT WORDS these sales people used to gain the trust of the potential customer.

After hundreds of interviews the researchers found that these top sales people used 5 phrases to gain confidence.

After the information was discovered the sales managers were instructed to have every sales person in the entire organization memorize these five powerful concepts.

At sales meetings they would randomly select a sales person and ask them to recite one of the phrases. They continued this program until it was a habit used by every sales person.

Needless to say, their sales reflected the use of the program.

Here they are:

1. "You get me. When you buy from The 3M Company you have to take me as part of the deal. I go with the package. And if you don't think I can make a difference – try me."

2. "Before I answer I want to make sure I understand what you are saying."

3. "If, at any time during this interview, I give you the feeling I am more interested in what I get out of this than I am in what you get out of it, just ask me to leave, I deserve it."

4. "I know how you feel, others have felt the same way, but after they tried it for the trial period they found it more than met their expectations."

5. "If this makes sense, is there any reason why we can't get started right now?"

Building trust is always the most important part of the sales process – especially when your competitors have most of the same products you have.

When a prospect is considering a new vendor you are one of several competitors. You present, others present, and buyers take their time to make the decision. Throughout this kind of sale, from the first call to the final presentation, building credibility plays a big role.

If you say "You get me," you have a good opportunity to prove it. Building credibility during the sales process can make or break the sale – many times it is what the decision is based on. And especially when there is time between asking for the business and getting the order, it is important to stay close to your customer. Telephone calls, letters, or personal visits can put you ahead of less attentive competitors.

Many salespeople are poor at taking care of this type of detail. Credibility is also a success factor after the sale to keep the business. Call or visit in between deliveries to find out how things are going.

Meeting and exceeding customer expectations will allow you to move up from vendor to partner.

How well you deliver on your sales promise will build your reputation with your customer and his or her colleagues.

Consider yourself successful if you learn in time that things are not going well. Credibility plays an important role, once the sale is in place, to help insure nothing goes wrong. After the sale, make sure it's not your last order with this customer.

One of the best ways to gain credibility with a prospect is to promise to do something-and then do it.

A customer will usually tell you about your competitors – "He is the best and I can always count on him" or "that guy lies to me and never calls me back when I need him". Sad to say that there are many "salespeople" who do not have the right 'ammunition" to be successful, whether it is morals, endurance or likeability. Learn what means the most to your customer, positively and negatively.

Crocker Smith

Something that I learned from a previous employer was called the LEAR model. Listen, Explore, Acknowledge and Respond. I use this model throughout the sales process and I have seen it work in building credibility with my clients. I like to ensure that I'm building a relationship that moves from being a vendor to a trusted advisor. Credibility isn't something you gain on the first visit but something that is established as you move from being the vendor to partner to finally the trusted advisor. Once you become the trusted advisor your credibility has already been proven.

Becky Akins

Warming up to the potential client is a huge part in selling. A lot of sales people walk in and begin their pitch, but I sincerely believe in warming up and getting to know the client for at least 10 minutes or so. In doing this you are not only getting to know you potential client, but you are selling yourself to them and building a trusting relationship. Let them know your there for them and to help fill their needs. And most of all, always follow through and follow up with whatever you tell them your going to do. If you let them know you're a man or woman of your word, chances are they will do business with you and continue that business for a long time.

David Bradley

Of all the products, ideas, and services one can sell, nothing is as important as selling oneself. There are thousands of people who can get the same product, or do the same service as I can, but they are not me. No two people are alike, and what makes one salesperson different from another is how well they can get people to "buy them". One of my sales mentors was a man named Mike Nerowski. He was about the hardest, meanest old SOB that I've ever met. But when he was in front of a customer, he was like a mother with a newborn baby. People loved him from the first 30 seconds that he was across from them. He would say the exact same "sales phrases" that I had already said to them, but in the end, he would get the sale, and usually get more for the same product that I was selling. Every customer is different, and it is up to us as salespeople to get them to like us, and to do whatever it takes to sell ourselves.

Barney Trader

"Bob, this may sound odd, but usually I don't try to sell anything at the first meeting with a prospect. We talk. I explain who we are, what we do, and then ask then to tell me about themselves and their business. By the time I leave, I know what they do, what they have done in the past, all about their children and grandchildren, etc. I leave information and a catalog of all that we offer and ask for a second meeting. At the second meeting, I have an idea of what products or programs might be beneficial to them, I've seem the space they have to work with, and they have had time to look over our product lines. Sometimes, I don't ask for a second meeting. Not everyone will have a need for what we do, and if I don't feel we are a good match, I don't hesitate to say so.

Either way, I always leave my card and point out that the number on the card is my cell number and they should call me at any time at that number if I can be of service...no automated system here. They call, I answer."

Cee Coats

"It's nice to know the key phrases that successful sales people use. But I don't think it's something you can say as a canned phrase - it has to be something that you really mean. A lot of people can tell when you are being sincere when you say something, so putting sincerity into those words will go a long way. I think the most important thing is to own those words, and make them into who you are.

Then selling yourself as part of the package for a partnership will fall into place."

Jo Welch

"So true! If you are not "scripted" when you walk in to see a new potential customer you are going in unprepared. Most people think that this is acting and not being yourself. On the contrary if you rehearse the script enough it will be yours. At any point in meeting a new customer I know what I will say and what I won't say. This builds confidence in what I DO say. If you truly mean and believe what your saying then it will sound sincere. The only thing I believe is critical at that point is doing what you say you will do and making them feel that they are one of your most important customers that you have....because they are!"

Dwayne Mitchell

About the author Bob Oros

Regardless of whether you are reading one of his books or attending one of his programs, the most frequent comment is: "This guy has been there, he is one of us, I am going to use these strategies."

With over 2,000 speaking engagements in all 50 states and several international locations for manufacturers, distributors and associations, you can be sure you will get the results and information you are looking for. Prior to starting his speaking career, Bob served six years in the US Navy as a Communications Specialist and then worked his way from a street sales person to the position of National Sales Manager for a Fortune 200 company.

Bob has received awards for speaking, writing and marketing too numerous to mention.

Additional Topics by Bob Oros

The Key to Selling Anybody

The Power of Expectations

Add Value to Every Product

Never Make the First Offer

How to Justify Your Price

Lost in 60 Seconds

One Good Reason to Buy

Control a Buyer's Attitude

Smoke Screen Objections

Take the Risk Out of Sales

How Small Companies Get Big